SIRIUS

This edition published in 2026 by Sirius Publishing, a division of
Arcturus Publishing Limited,
26/27 Bickels Yard, 151–153 Bermondsey Street,
London SE1 3HA

ISBN: 978-1-3988-5315-7
AD011856NT
Supplier 24, Date 1225, PI00012985

Printed in Malaysia